# THE REST
# IS HISTORY

## Extraordinary Antics
## of People in History

MARK SEAMAN

**PAST TIMES**™
Oxford, England

Special Edition for PAST TIMES™, Oxford, England

First published in this format in Great Britain in 1996 by
Michael O'Mara Books Limited
9 Lion Yard
Tremadoc Road
London SW4 7NQ

A CIP catalogue record of this book is available from the British Library

ISBN 1-85479-628-3

Designed by Mick Keates
Typesetting by Concise Artisans
Printed in Hong Kong by Midas Printing Co.

*Picture acknowledgements:*
Peter Newark's Military Pictures: 7, 9, 20, 26, 24, 33, 36, 40,
60, 65, 69, 76; Popperfoto: title page, 5, 10, 12, 13, 14, 15, 25, 30 (top),
32, 35, 39, 41, 45, 51, 57, 71, 74, 82; Robin Marsh: 16; Bridgeman Art
Library: 17, 21, 28, 37, 49, 53, 56, 61, 68, 72, 80, 81, 85, 86, 88;
The Fotomas Index: 18, 23, 30 (bottom), 43, 66, 75.

Title page: *Kaiser Wilhelm II went to great lengths to personify the
Prussian war-lord. He was rarely photographed out of uniform,
always unsmiling and usually striking a pose of disdainful resolution.
But the image was flawed. His belligerent stance disguised the fact that
his left arm was crippled. Electric treatment merely hurt the patient,
adding one more neurosis to a person who was to build up an
impressive collection by maturity.*

# CONTENTS

# QUOTATIONS

*'We taught that goddam horse of yours a lesson.'*

This telephone message was communicated by 'Two Gun' Louis Alterie, a member of Chicago's O'Banion gang, during the Prohibition. The horse in question was held responsible for the death of a popular hoodlum, Samuel J. 'Nails' Morton, who had been killed in a riding accident. The grief-stricken gangsters hired the miscreant from the stables, led it to the scene of its misdemeanour and ceremonially executed it, with each member of the gang firing a bullet into the horse's head. The deed done, Alterie informed the stable's owner that revenge had been exacted.

*'My family give me no help. They are all insanely ambitious, ruinously extravagant and devoid of talent.'*

Napoleon's words merely echo the moans of disgruntled dynasts heard since the first tribe had a chief. But the French Emperor had good cause for dissatisfaction, having gone out of his way to keep the fruits of his triumphs in the family, only to find that they became bruised with mishandling. He gave his elder brother, Joseph, the throne of Spain, but he proved to be an abject failure, borrowing money from France when Napoleon intended him to put Spanish gold in the Imperial coffers. Two of his other

*A morose Napoleon contemplates the vicissitudes of family life*

brothers, Jérôme and Louis, were crowned Kings of Westphalia and Holland respectively, both were a disappointment. Jérôme was only interested in the easy life of royal pageantry and in his several mistresses, while Louis quarrelled with Napoleon, abdicated and went to Austria. The Emperor's remaining brother, Lucien, also fell out with him. He set off for America but was captured *en route* by the British, and spent the rest of the Napoleonic Wars in rustic contentment in Worcestershire. Faced with the prospect of entrusting his succession to one of his clan, Napoleon was obliged to undertake the distressing course of divorcing his wife, Josephine, and marrying the daughter of the Emperor of Austria. The marriage took place in April 1810 and, in March the next year, a delighted Napoleon had a son.

*'Nobody shot me.'*

This firm denial was made by the Chicago mobster Frank Gusenburg, who had the dubious distinction of being the only victim of the infamous St. Valentine's Day Massacre to be still alive when the police arrived on the scene. Bleeding from fourteen bullet wounds, Gusenburg was rushed to hospital while detectives pressed him for information as to the identities of his assailants. Gusenburg offered the above statement, adding rather redundantly 'I ain't no copper', and then died.

*Some of Frank Gusenberg's fellow victims after the St. Valentine's Day Massacre*

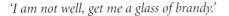

*'I am not well, get me a glass of brandy.'*

One could quite understandably expect this quotation to have been the dying words of an alcoholic, but they are not. In fact, they were uttered by George, Prince of Wales, the eldest son of King George III, in April 1795, upon the occasion of his first meeting with his bride-to-be. Having been coerced into getting married (for reasons of state and relieving his debts), the Prince had made a dreadful choice. His fiancée, Caroline, Princess of Brunswick, was dirty, rarely changed her linen, stank, swore, was eccentric to the point of madness, and was sexually promiscuous (it was rumoured that she had spent the night on deck alone with the first mate of the ship that brought her to England). The only way that the Prince could get through the marriage ceremony was to be in a state of advanced intoxication, which also perhaps explains his consummation of their union on their wedding night. But once was enough. Although the 'happy couple' lived in the same house, they only communicated in writing until they separated a few months later.

*'It eases my mind to know that while I'm away the tides will be very unfavourable for a landing. Besides, air reconnaissance gives no reason to think it's imminent.'*

This parting comment was made by Field-Marshal Erwin Rommel to his naval adviser on 5 June 1944. Germany's celebrated 'Desert Fox' was bidding his staff farewell as he left for a well-deserved leave at home, assuring them that the long-awaited invasion was not about to happen. He was wrong. Later that same night, as Rommel drove homewards, thousands of Allied airborne troops landed in Normandy, followed later the next day by the biggest invasion the world had ever seen.

*'Ce bougre-là a quitté ici avec ses culottes pleines de merde.'*

A very free twentieth-century translation of the above might be rendered: 'The little shit has done a runner.' The 'little shit' in question was Napoleon

Bonaparte and he had 'run away' from Egypt in August 1799, after an uncharacteristically disastrous campaign in the Middle East. It was the circumstances of his departure that inspired this vitriolic comment from General Kléber, who had only learnt of Napoleon's decision to return to France when he found a note appointing him as the new commander. Kléber's inheritance was a small, sick army, which was seven million francs in debt, and cut off from France by the Royal Navy's blockade. It was to his credit that Kléber made the best of a bad job and was quite successful, until he was assassinated by a Moslem fanatic. His successor, General Menou, was not as able a soldier but had the advantage of being a supreme realist. He became a Moslem and, when all hope of relief from France was at an end, he negotiated terms of surrender with the British that allowed him to take the remnants of his army home.

*Napoleon orders his troops to the Pyramids while he promptly beats a hasty retreat back to Paris*

*'It makes no difference, he has enough for all.'*

This was Mrs Rasputin's endearingly tolerant and realistic response to comments about her husband's notorious extra-marital affairs.

*The 'Mad Monk' enjoying the company of some of his admirers*

*'How amused the servants would be to find us in bed together.'*

The naive wedding-night comment of the Grand Duke Peter to his young bride. In fact, Peter was more than just an innocent, being somewhat retarded, both physically and mentally. While her husband contented himself by playing with toy soldiers, his highly sexed wife, the future Catherine the Great, grew ever more frustrated. The unhappy couple probably remained virgins for the next seven years until Catherine took a lover and Peter had an operation carried out on his genitals. The results were immediate, if confusing: Catherine had a miscarriage and her husband took a mistress. Although Peter's rehabilitation was such that the two occasionally slept together, it is probable that he remained sterile and that the child born to Catherine in 1754 was fathered by her lover, Saltykov.

*'If I didn't have my hair curled every day I couldn't enjoy my food.'*

There was a history of madness in the Bavarian ruling dynasty that reached its peak with King Ludwig II, who was responsible for the above statement. Distinctly odd for most of his twenty-two-year reign, his eccentricity steadily became more pronounced, manifesting itself most obviously in a string of fairy-tale castles and palaces built throughout his alpine kingdom. Having indulged himself with such antics as reversing night and day, inviting his horse to dinner, and providing his palace guard with sofas to stave off fatigue when on duty, Ludwig was finally declared insane and deposed by his uncle. Sadly, the peaceful lunatic was not allowed to live out his days in one of his architectural triumphs. Shortly after a regency had been declared, he was found drowned in a shallow lake. The mystery of his death was further deepened when the corpse of his doctor was fished out of the water shortly afterwards.

*Al Capone in uncharacteristically jovial mood*

*'I've been accused of every death except the casualty list of the World War.'*

Was Al Capone's response to newspaper reports of his involvement in Chicago's gang wars of the Prohibition era. His exaggeration was a heavy-handed attempt to camouflage some rather incriminating statistics. Between 1927 and 1931 when Capone was indisputable head of Chicago's underworld, there were 227 gang murders in the city. Furthermore, Capone was thought to have personally killed between twenty and sixty men and to have ordered the murder of at least 400 others during his career. It is interesting to note that he was never charged with any of these homocides.

# MADNESS AND ECCENTRICITY

THE EMPEROR CALIGULA was well received by the people of Rome when he succeeded the dissipated Tiberius, but they soon changed their minds. At first Caligula's odd behaviour only affected the Imperial court, who became the victims of his whims and insane plans. Senators had to behave like slaves and trot alongside Caligula's chariot, relatives who might be potential rivals for the throne were ordered to commit suicide, and brides at society weddings ran the risk of being abducted in the middle of the ceremony if the Emperor took a fancy to them. Caligula managed to possess just about all the character disorders in the psychiatrist's textbook, revelling in his power and indulging his sadism with comments to his executioner such as 'Strike him so that he feels he is dying.' And the mad Emperor did not confine himself to projects solely within the palace walls; Caligula delighted in schemes whose only justification

*The public face of the private madman*

was perversity. Thus harbours were constructed at places where the sea was at its deepest, tunnels were mined through solid rock, mountains were flattened, and plains were transformed into mountains. This lunacy was tolerated for four years, before the Emperor was assassinated by his bodyguard, whose actions for once reflected popular sentiment.

FIELD-MARSHAL PRINCE VON BLÜCHER was Prussia's leading general during the Napoleonic wars, his greatest victory being achieved as commander of his country's troops at the Battle of Waterloo. He was somewhat mentally unbalanced and was very fond of a tipple, which had the combined effect of making him prone to bouts of insanity and eccentric behaviour. In 1809 he became convinced that he was pregnant as a result of having been raped by a French soldier. His lunatic fantasy was completed by his conviction that his offspring would be an elephant. This French connection continued into his persecution mania. He believed Napoleon's agents lit fires under the floorboards of his quarters so that they were too hot to walk upon. His solution to this problem was to cross the room by leaping from one piece of furniture to another.

*Blücher's horse chooses a decidedly inappropriate moment to express his feelings during the battle of Ligny*

*Lieutenant-Colonel Kitchener, the father of the somewhat more famous Field-Marshal*

THE FAMOUS SOLDIER and statesman, Lord Kitchener, was a very straitlaced person, perhaps as a result of his father's eccentricity. Kitchener senior, a former army officer, held many strange opinions on a host of subjects, including a distrust of schools, which rendered his son virtually illiterate until his early teens. His oddest theory was that blankets were unhealthy and should be replaced as bedclothes by old newspapers, which he considered were cheap, clean and just as effective. He therefore had sheets of *The Times* sewn together and hung across his bed, suspending them from boards constructed around the bedframe. Initially he had wanted to sleep wrapped in paper but Mrs Kitchener complained that the rustling would keep her awake at night. Mr Kitchener would surely have been forgiven if he had replied that at least he had furnished her with something to read during her bouts of insomnia.

◆

KING GEORGE III, who reigned from 1760 to 1820, was for lengthy periods quite mad. Historians have detected the first signs of insanity as early as 1765, but it was in October 1788 that the 'flying gout' truly

*A moment of culinary repose from the 'flying gout' for George III*

took a grip. The King's physical condition deteriorated, he developed insomnia and suffered acute
delirium that made him talk rapidly and incessantly.
And his state of mind was scarcely helped by the bar-
baric medical 'treatment' to which he was subjected.
Amongst the so-called remedies were irritants
applied to his legs to draw away the 'humours', but

which merely served to hurt him, prevent sleep and increase irritability. Understandably, the King removed them and, for his pains, was put in a strait-jacket by his doctors. Although the King made a recovery, it was by no means permanent and he suffered recurrent relapses as he grew older. For the last years of his life, George spent most of his time wandering in the gardens of his palaces, blind, deaf and talking to trees.

◆

PETER THE GREAT liked to use his absolute power to indulge his own bizarre sense of humour. He took pleasure in embarrassing the nobility, using common people as pawns in his practical jokes. By sponsoring his servants' weddings, he invoked all the

*Peter the Great – Tsar and arch-prankster*

paraphenalia and ceremony of high society but added spice to the affair by employing a collection of freaks to carry out official duties. Invitations were entrusted to chronic stutterers and the footmen, whose task was to run alongside the carriages, were the fattest men he could find. To cap the occasion, the priest selected to officiate at the wedding was blind, deaf and as drunk as Peter and the guests.

◆

ON THE SURFACE, Sir Thomas More, Lord Chancellor of England, was one of Europe's most intelligent and cultivated men but he was also racked by self-doubt and sexual repression. Although his original intention was to be a priest, More realised

*Spot the man in the horse-hair shirt – Sir Thomas More seated in the bosom of his family*

when still a youth that the laws of celibacy were not for him. But this did not make him a libertine. On the contrary, his two marriages were singularly devoid of physical or intellectual attraction and his homelife was positively puritanical. He also punished himself for his weakness by self-flagellation (carried out in a shed at the bottom of his garden) and by wearing a horse-hair shirt of more than ordinary unpleasantness.

KING HENRY VI of England could scarcely have been less like his father, Henry V, the victor of Agincourt. The younger Henry never had a chance to imitate his heroic parent as Henry senior died when his son was only nine months old. As the boy grew up his kingdom steadily disintegrated, at roughly the same rate as his mind deteriorated. He became a religious obsessive and completely lost touch with the ways of his courtiers. By his late teens, the sight of a low-cut gown was so distressing to him that he was moved to run screaming from the room at the approach of a well-endowed lady-in-waiting.

IT IS COMMON KNOWLEDGE that H.M. Stanley found David Livingstone in the heart of the African jungle, introducing himself with the famous presumption. But having made contact once more with

*The beginning of a legend – a popular biography of Livingstone published soon after his death*

the outside world, what happened to Livingstone? The reason for his apparent relapse into obscurity is simple: Livingstone had completed virtually all his major explorations and his ruined health prevented him from undertaking any more really taxing expeditions. He did spend several months exploring with Stanley after their meeting in November 1871, but a renewed attack of dysentery early in 1873 forced him to curtail his travels. The missionary-explorer died in Africa in May 1873, aged sixty, appropriately kneeling in prayer at the side of his bed.

♦

MOST PEOPLE'S KNOWLEDGE of William Bligh ends when he was dumped in a small boat by the *Bounty*'s mutineers and told to find his own way

*Captain Bligh makes his opinion felt to the mutineers as he embarks upon his epic journey*

home. But although Bligh was tactless, harsh and severe, he was a superb sailor and managed to sail his boat (together with a crew of loyal seamen) some 4,000 miles to safety. Contrary to expectations, his career did not unduly suffer from the loss of the *Bounty*. But lightning was to strike twice more. In 1797 Bligh's new command, HMS *Director*, mutinied. Once again, he bounced back, and was appointed Governor of New South Wales. Sadly, his well-known character traits led to a particularly stormy period in office, and he found himself confronted by a third mutiny arising from his 'oppressive behaviour'. But the Admiralty still saw his disciplinarian attitude as an asset rather than a liability, and Bligh had attained the elevated rank of Vice-Admiral before his death in 1817, aged sixty-three.

LIKE MANY FASHION SETTERS, Beau Brummell's rise was meteoric and his fall profound. While affecting lowly origins, George Bryan Brummell had been to Eton and Oxford and, although not of the aristocracy, his charm, wit and, above all, elegance made him the leader of London's young society in the 1800s. But after a decade as the close friend of the Prince of Wales and leading a lifestyle of unrelenting extravagance, Brummell had burnt himself out. He fell out with his royal disciple and slipped so heavily into debt that, in 1816, he fled to France in order to escape his creditors. His decline continued and he was finally imprisoned for his debts, this time run up in Normandy. Now in his fifties and far from the handsome Regency buck of yesteryear, his health gave way. In 1837 he was committed to a lunatic asylum at Caen and died there in March 1840.

*Beau Brummell sacrificing elegance for warmth*

IN 1881 PAT GARRETT shot and killed Billy the Kid. It brought the lawman instant fame but little else. He had to take legal action to get his reward money and lost his job as sheriff. There followed a period of travel throughout the South-West, working on ranches, in law enforcement, and even as a collector of customs at El Paso (a job arranged for him by President Theodore Roosevelt). Finally, in 1908, Garrett's colourful life was brought to an abrupt close. He got into an argument with Wayne Brazil, a tenant who was ranching his land for him, and in the ensuing fracas Garrett was shot in the head and stomach. Brazil was, nevertheless, able to enter a successful plea of self-defence when sent to trial.

*Pat Garrett, right, and his victim, Billy the Kid*

FOLLOWING HIS SUCCESS in the American Civil War, General Ulysses Simpson Grant stayed at the forefront of his country's affairs for more than a decade. When the war finished he became Secretary of State for War and, in 1868, began the first of his two terms as President of the United States. Sadly,

Grant was no politician and the next eight years were dominated by economic depression, monetary scandals and governmental corruption. Grant retired from politics in 1877 and devoted himself to a business career that was, if anything, even more calamitous than his presidency. He had

*General Grant during his hey-day in the American Civil War and before his less than successful move into politics*

become heavily involved in the founding of a banking house, so when this went bankrupt in 1884, his personal finances were ruined. Sick, poor and having lost everything, Grant set about writing his memoirs to provide a future source of income for his wife. With the help of Mark Twain as his publisher, Grant won his last battle and, after his death from cancer of the throat in 1885, his widow was left financially secure.

THE LADY WITH THE LAMP is one of the best-known images of Victorian England, second only to the Queen herself. Florence Nightingale's work during the Crimean War helped to foster the development of military medicine and professional nursing and, more than a century later, earned her a distinguished place on the back of a ten-pound note. After the war, her career was dominated by her campaigns for medical reform throughout the Empire.

*The lady without her lamp, Florence Nightingale, seated, with her sister*

She never married, and led a highly active life until her mid-seventies when she took to her bedroom for good. Her sight had troubled her since 1867 and, by the late 1880s, she was virtually blind, while her mind also began to fail. For the last four years of her life she was all but comatose, experiencing ever-lengthening periods of unconsciousness. Finally in August 1910, the farce ended and she passed away at the not inconsiderable age of ninety years and three months.

THE ASSASSINATION of the Archduke Franz Ferdinand at Sarajevo in June 1914 was the flashpoint that led to the outbreak of the First World War. Naturally enough, the world's attention was diverted away from the small Balkan town and the fate of the assassins. Gavrilo Princip, the man who fired the shots, and twenty-four of his fellow conspirators were arrested and put on trial. Sixteen were found guilty, of whom three were executed. Princip and several others, however, were still juveniles and, as a result, were spared the death penalty. Princip and two others died of tuberculosis in prison during the war that they had helped to begin. Two of the conspirators who were released after the war ironically pursued careers that gave them ample opportunity to reflect upon their roles in history: one became Professor of History at Belgrade University, and the other later held the post of Curator at Sarajevo's museum.

# ASSASSINATIONS AND MURDERS

NERO'S LOVE LIFE was more than a little bit complicated, but he had in his power the means to simplify it – murder. Although he had a wife and many mistresses, the dominant woman in Nero's life was his mother, Agrippina, who had ruthlessly masterminded her son's path to the Imperial throne. But steadily, as his self-confidence grew, Nero became less dependent upon Agrippina. Independence changed to antagonism when he decided that he wanted to divorce his wife and marry his mistress, Poppaea Sabina. Agrippina refused to sanction the

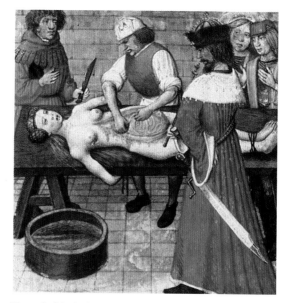

*The end of Agrippina – a gruesome medieval impression of the murder of Nero's mother*

change in her son's domestic arrangements, so Nero resolved to kill his mother. As an old hand at administering poison, Agrippina was too wily to be killed off by that method. Nero therefore lured her on to a ship and then had it sunk; Agrippina, however, survived the shipwreck and managed to swim ashore. Now subtlety was dispensed with, and a gang of assassins raided Agrippina's villa and stabbed her to death. There only remained Nero's wife, Octavia, as an impediment of the realisation of her husband's plans, but she proved as stubborn as her mother-in-law had been. Nero's answer was to sentence her to death on trumped-up charges of infidelity, and although his men were unable to bleed Octavia to death, they asphyxiated her in a steambath. But marriage to Poppaea was, in the end, not all sweetness and light. One day, in a fit of rage, Nero kicked his pregnant wife in the stomach and killed her.

◆

THE TWENTIETH CENTURY has no monopoly of revolutions and assassination plots. Even in the supposed calm and stability of Georgian England an ambitious plot was laid to overthrow the monarchy and government. Led by Arthur Thistlewood, the illegitimate son of a Lincolnshire farmer, a conspiracy was formed to dethrone George IV and proclaim a republic. The first step was to be the murder of the entire Cabinet who, propitiously, were scheduled to dine together on 23 February 1820 at Lord

*The target, George IV, and the would-be assassins*

Harrowby's house in Grosvenor Square. Having disposed of the government in one fell swoop, the conspirators anticipated little problem in seizing control of London. While the plan for widespread revolution was hare-brained, the assassination plot was quite practical. But as is frequently the case, the conspirators' security was non-existent and the authorities soon knew of their intentions. Lord Harrowby's dinner party was cancelled and a force of police and soldiers raided the revolutionaries' hideout in Cato Street, off the Edgware Road. A violent and confused affray ensued, during which Thistlewood killed a constable before making his escape with several of the gang. He was, however, captured the next day and, with the wheels of justice running abnormally fast, was hanged outside Newgate Gaol in May 1820.

◆

ON 30 JUNE 1934 Hitler carried out a purge of the Nazi Party, eliminating dissidents and disposing of embarrassments. His main target was the SA, a paramilitary force that he now saw as a threat to his own authority. Its leader, Ernst Röhm, was arrested and generously given the opportunity to take his own life. After ten minutes of sitting in his cell with a loaded pistol, SS guards went in and helped Röhm out, shooting him three times in the chest and head. In the course of the purge, known as the 'Night of the Long Knives', others were not to be treated so respectfully: SA Obergruppenfuehrer Heines was

*Hitler takes the salute of his SA before he unleashes the 'Night of the Long Knives'*

arrested when in bed with a young man and, along with other senior SA men, was put up against a wall and shot. Old scores were settled, such as when the man who had defeated Hitler's 1923 Putsch was beaten to death and his body dumped on a heath. In the mayhem mistakes were inevitably made and Willi Schmid, the music critic, received the bullets intended for Willi Schmidt. But perhaps the most poignant episode of the purge involved Karl Ernst, one of Röhm's most trusted confederates. Ernst had just got married and was about to begin his honeymoon with a sea cruise when the SS caught up with him. Instead of a voyage on a luxury liner, Ernst went on a one-way trip to Berlin.

JAMES BUTLER HICKOK, better known as 'Wild Bill Hickok', was one of the Wild West's most deadly gunmen. By 1876, though, he was slowing down and, not unnaturally, it worried him. The man who had driven stagecoaches, fought in the Civil War and against the Indians, later tried his hand at starring in a Wild West Show, but he did not like the life and went west again. He made his way to Deadwood City, troubled by failing eyesight and having suffered, three years earlier, the distressing experience of reading his own obituary published in the *Missouri Democrat*. On 2 August 1876 he was sitting in Carl Mann's saloon playing poker with some friends when Jack McCall walked in and shot him in

*Jack McCall pays his respects to 'Wild Bill Hickok'*

the head. There seemed little reason for the murder, though it has been alleged that McCall was a hired assassin. The alternative explanation is that the murderer had lost to Hickok at poker earlier that day and was probably drunk when he exacted his revenge. Usually Hickok would have been prepared for such an attack by taking a seat facing the door with his back to the wall, but a friend had jokingly refused to let him have his regular place, thereby giving McCall his chance. The killer was arrested, tried and, incredibly, acquitted. A retrial was ordered, however, and this time McCall was found guilty, and hanged in March 1877.

THE NOSE HAVE IT, or if you have to be assassinated, it is always handy to have a couple of hundred surgeons around. In April 1926, the Italian dictator, Benito Mussolini, attended the opening ceremony of an international congress of surgeons. As the strains of the Fascist national anthem were struck up, Il Duce stopped in his tracks and snapped to attention. At that very moment a shot rang out. The assailant was Violet Gibson, a sixty-two-year-old Irishwoman who had come to Rome to shoot either Mussolini or the Pope. Mussolini turned out to be her would-be victim, but her success was limited. The dictator's sudden movement had spoilt Violet's aim and, instead of blowing his head off, the point-blank shot had merely grazed Mussolini's nose. Scarcely extending the surgical repertoire of the congress, Mussolini was soon able to continue his official duties with a strip of sticking plaster across his nose to bear witness to the attempt on his life. As for Miss Gibson, she was magnanimously freed on her victim's orders, and deported.

*The assassin leaves her mark*

VICTIMS OF ASSASSINATION do not as a rule show a willingness to assist their would-be killers, but Rasputin was positively bad-mannered in the trouble to which he put his murderers.

*Prince Felix Yousoupoff, the long-suffering assassin of Rasputin*

In December 1916 Rasputin was invited to the house of a 'friend'. There he was fed poisoned cakes and wine but, with the cyanide having little or no effect, he was then shot. The assassins left the 'body' only to find on their return that it had moved. So Rasputin was shot again, beaten with an iron bar, kicked, tied up and thrown into the River Neva. But the 'Mad Monk's' tribulations were not over – for he was still alive when they dumped him in the water. When the body was eventually fished out of the river by the authorities, an autopsy was carried out and revealed that the cause of death was drowning. A year later, the Bolsheviks dug up Rasputin's body from his grave and burnt it in what was supposedly a symbolic act, but, in the light of his previous stubborn refusal to die, perhaps the revolutionaries were simply not taking any chances.

IN FEBRUARY 1933 an attempt was made on the life of President F.D. Roosevelt in Miami, Florida. A deranged anarchist, Giuseppi Zangara, fired several shots at the President's entourage but the only casualty was Toni Cermak, the Mayor of Chicago, who received a fatal wound in the stomach. It was later

*Ten years after Zangara's assassination attempt, FDR was still going strong*

ruled that Zangara was not sufficiently insane to escape the death penalty and he was sent to the electric chair. But, as is so often the case with assassinations, that is not the end of the story. It has now come to light that Cermak was not an innocent victim but was the target of a second, mystery gunman. Zangara's gun was a .32 calibre whilst the bullets that hit the Mayor were from a .45. Historians have conjectured that a hitman had been given a contract by Al Capone to kill Cermak and that Zangara's failure to kill the President was a convenient diversion for the gangster's success.

THERE WERE SO MANY attempts to assassinate Tsar Alexander II that he developed a reputation as a one-man disaster area. To be anywhere in his vicinity was felt to be so hazardous that the citizens of St. Petersburg would not buy tickets for the opera unless they were given an assurance that the Tsar was not attending the performance. Finally, in March 1881, the assassins succeeded. A bomb was thrown at the Imperial cortège and exploded, injuring a child and a cossack guardsman but leaving the Tsar unharmed. Alexander ordered his carriage to stop and went to comfort the wounded man when a second bomb was flung. This time twenty spectators were killed and the Tsar was almost blown in half. He died about an hour later.

*Alexander obligingly leaves his carriage and thereby helps the assassin to complete the job*

---

FEW OF THE OUTLAWS of the Wild West died in a shoot-out. A very subdued fate befell the most famous of all the bandits: Jesse James. A $10,000 reward put on the outlaw's head inspired Charlie and Bob Ford to travel to St. Joseph, Missouri, where James was living with his wife and two children. At 8 o'clock in the morning of 3 April 1882, the two brothers approached James's house. Inside, the out-law was standing on a chair, straightening a picture.

There was no attempt at an arrest. Bob Ford shot Jesse James in the back of the head, whilst his brother stood by as witness and look-out. It was the end of the notorious bandit but the beginning of his murderer's career as a celebrity. Ford, a man of dubious background, now began an itinerant life throughout the west, performing in stage shows as 'The Man Who Shot Jesse James'. His less than heroic deed made him generally unpopular with audiences and it was only when he became a saloon owner in New Mexico and Colorado that he attained any form of success. But violence still surrounded him and in 1892 Ford got on the wrong end of a shotgun blast, his killer receiving little notoriety and a twenty-year sentence.

*Jesse James, the apprentice outlaw, when a $10,000 reward and a bullet in the back of his head seemed a world away*

MUCH OF ADOLF HITLER'S popularity in Germany relied on his image as the Reich's father figure. It was therefore essential that his love affairs be carried out with tact and secrecy but twice his image was only preserved at the price of his lovers' lives. The first, Geli Raubal, ostensibly committed suicide in September 1931 by shooting herself with Hitler's pistol. The second girl, Renate Muller, died in 1937 after a short illness brought on by being thrown out of a window. Having taken Hitler as a lover, both committed the unpardonable sins of taking another man and that man being a Jew. Needless to say, the facts are hazy both as to the exact circumstances of their deaths and their relationships with Hitler but their stories could have shattered the conventional picture of Hilter's private life.

*Hitler arranges a date*

## BLUNDERS

IN APRIL 1918 Commander Ernest Boyce thought that he had pulled off a great coup. Boyce, the head of the British Secret Intelligence Service's operations in Russia, had acquired some vital documents that revealed the Bolsheviks' true relations with Germany. Admittedly Boyce had spent a small fortune in purchasing the papers, but they clearly proved that Lenin and Trotsky were German agents and that the Russian revolutionaries were in close contact with the German General Staff. The documents were passed onto two experts who promptly pronounced them fakes, pointing out that the papers, ostensibly a collection from sources throughout Russia, had all been typed on one machine. Staring failure and disgrace squarely in the face, Boyce did the only thing he could do. He sold the documents to the United States Mission in Petrograd for a sizeable profit.

◆

IN 1879 a British army invaded Zululand and a base camp was set up at Isandhlwana, from which the expedition's commander set out to look for the main Zulu army. Unfortunately, while Lord Chelmsford was out looking for them, 20,000 Zulus found his camp. At first, the disciplined fire of the British infantry held off the massed attacks of the enemy. Soon, however, the riflemen began to run out of ammunition. Runners were sent from the firing line to fetch more cartridges, but even in the heat of battle bureaucracy reared its stubborn head. There were ample stocks of ammunition, but many of the quartermasters refused to issue cartridges to men who were not from their own units. To make matters worse, the ammunition was packed in heavy wooden boxes, sealed by metal bands and with the lids held down by screws. Not only did they find that the screws were invariably rusted into the wood, but there were simply not enough screwdrivers. Valuable time was lost while the soldiers tried to prise open the boxes and get at their precious contents. Inevitably, the redcoats' fire slackened and the Zulus closed in. Without ammunition, it was a case of too few bayonets against too many assegais – barely 350 survived out of the British force of 1,800 men.

*The aftermath of the disaster – British troops survey the field of battle at Isandhlwana*

NAPOLEON'S CAMPAIGN in Germany and Austria during the autumn and early winter of 1805 is a testament to his military brilliance. This is not to say that the French Emperor was not ably assisted by the glaring inadequacies of his Russian and Austrian adversaries. At Austerlitz, Napoleon cleverly lured his opponents to attack him while he defended a strong position. The night before the battle, the Austrian general, Weyrother, in conference with his fellow commanders, outlined a long and complex plan that relied heavily upon the French conforming precisely to his predictions. As Weyrother spoke, the Russian commander, Kutusov, was fast asleep. Further problems occurred with the slowness of making a Russian translation of the Austrian battle plan. It was not until 3 a.m. on the morning of the battle that the orders began to be circulated throughout the army. The delay resulted in some of the Russian units failing to receive their instructions until after they were supposed to have moved. Thus the Austro-Russian army began the battle of Austerlitz in a state of ham-fisted confusion that was to end in total defeat and 26,000 casualties.

◆

WHEN THE ARMISTICE was signed in November 1918, the position of the German High Seas Fleet was decidedly unusual. It had avoided battle for most of the war, apart from Jutland and a few brief clashes in the North Sea, and at the time of the surrender it was still an intact, immensely powerful naval force. The conditions of the ceasefire dictated that the fleet be interned until the peace treaty was negotiated. An odd situation developed with over seventy German warships at anchor in the British base at Scapa Flow, watched over by the guns of the Royal Navy. Tension increased as the diplomats failed to find a quick solution to end the war. The German commander, Admiral Ludwig von Reuter, deprived of information and a sitting target if war was resumed, made secret arrangements to scuttle his fleet. Isolated in the Orkneys, von Reuter relied to a great extent upon old newspapers for information on the progress at the peace talks. Finally, on Saturday 21 June 1919,

*The man who sank more German ships than the Royal Navy – Admiral von Reuter*

on the day when the original armistice agreement expired, von Reuter gave the order for the fleet to scuttle. Before the Royal Navy could intervene, the Germans had opened the sea-cocks and sunk the ships. It seems unlikely that von Reuter was aware that the armistice had been extended by two more days, but it also seems certain that he had made a decision that the High Seas Fleet would never become a bargaining counter in the peace treaty.

THE RUSSO-JAPANESE WAR of 1904-5 was an unmitigated disaster for the Tsar's army and navy. The action took place in Manchuria, on Japan's doorstep but thousands of miles from Moscow and St. Petersburg. It was not long before Russia's land and sea forces were bottled up in Port Arthur, leaving Nicholas II and his government smarting under this massive blow to their Imperial dignity. The situation needed a grand gesture; all that was offered, however, was farce. It was decided that a relief force be sent, and the Russian Baltic Fleet was chosen for the job. A glance at the map would have shown that the 18,000-mile voyage around the world was impractical, while it was common knowledge in the navy that the Baltic Fleet was badly led, badly equipped, badly trained and riddled with revolutionary agitators. Nevertheless, the Fleet set sail in October 1904. All the worst fears were soon realised when it entered the North Sea and sank some of the Hull fishing fleet, nearly precipitating war with Great Britain and certain annihilation by the guns of the Royal Navy. Fortunately, the incident was smoothed over and the Russian armada sailed on around the continent of Africa. The Fleet was off the coast of Madagascar when news reached it that Port Arthur had fallen to the Japanese. But, in keeping with the lunacy that surrounded the whole enterprise, they were ordered to proceed to the Pacific. Miraculously, they arrived off Korea by the end of May 1905 – only to be pounced upon by the Japanese navy at Tsushima. The Baltic Fleet had sailed around the world only to be slaughtered, their sole achievement being to make St. Petersburg sue for peace.

GENERAL JOSÉ SANJURJO was a Spanish right-wing leader who went into exile in Portugal on the assumption of power by the Republican party. He should have stayed in his new home. Instead, he chose to organise a coup to overthrow the Spanish government. By 1932 his plans were laid and, understandably proud of them, it is reported that he confided his strategy to a prostitute during a moment of amorous respite. The details of the General's scheme were soon known in Madrid and the uprising was cancelled. Undismayed, Sanjurjo tried again in 1936, this time with closer security. A small aeroplane was prepared to fly him out of Portugal, but Spain's would-be saviour demanded that he be sartorially worthy of the occasion. Against the advice of his staff and the pilot, the aircraft was crammed full of the General's ceremonial uniforms. Not surprisingly, the aeroplane crashed on take-off, killing the fashion-conscious Sanjurjo.

# SEX

ONE OF THE COUNTLESS ALLIED PLANS to end the Second World War envisaged an air raid on Hitler's headquarters. At first glance, this does not seem a particularly original idea, except that this aerial bombardment was to consist of pornography, not high explosive. The American intelligence organisation, the Office of Strategic Services, employed a team of psychoanalysts who speculated that Hitler's psychological profile indicated that he might be an avid user of pornography. They therefore concluded that an inundation of lurid reading matter would either totally derange him or give him a heart attack. Huge stocks of pornographic material were collected and crates, designed to fly open on impact, were constructed. But the plan was finally abandoned due to 'shortage of aircraft' or an attack of common sense on the part of the OSS's commanding officers.

◆

THE EMPEROR TIBERIUS was fifty-six years old when he came to the throne. His life had been soured by violence and the need to repress his feelings, so that now, as absolute ruler of the Roman Empire, he indulged himself with abandon. As a bisexual, the range of his pleasures was vast, embracing a penchant for voyeurism and a partiality for oral sex performed by slave boys (his 'minnows') who swam with him in the baths. He made homosexual advances to temple attendants after a service and their refusal led to their legs being broken. He favoured the Isle of Capri as a hideaway from the cares of the state, but it was not a happy place for those who annoyed him as they were simply flung off the nearest cliff.

*The stern and unyielding face of Tiberius*

♦

COLONEL VALENTINE BAKER was one of Victorian England's finest cavalry officers. Commanding the famous 10th Hussars, he had introduced reforms in training and tactics that made him renowned and respected at home and abroad. Then, in 1875, he fell from grace. On 17 June a Miss Dickinson was seen clinging to the open door of a railway train as it sped between Walton and Esher. The train was stopped and the hysterical young woman said that she had been attacked by the man sitting opposite her in the compartment. That man was Valentine Baker. Amidst much public clamour, Colonel Baker was sent for trial on charges of assault with intent to ravage, indecent assault and common assault. Although it was basically just Miss Dickinson's word against the Colonel's, his claim that she took fright after misinterpreting a casual remark was rejected by the jury. He was sentenced to prison for twelve months, fined £500, and 'removed' from the Army. His career in England was ruined, but on his release Baker's undoubted military talents were not completely wasted, as he went on to serve with distinction in the Sultan of Turkey's army in the war against Russia and, later, as the commander of the Egyptian Gendarmerie. It is interesting to note that, in spite of his conviction, his old regiment and most of the military establishment retained a belief in his innocence. He was re-elected to the Army and Navy and Marlborough clubs, but his rehabilitation was never complete. A brilliant career had been ruined either by a moment's lust or a neurotic girl's imagination.

THE EMPRESS ELIZABETH, daughter of Peter the Great, certainly maintained the family tradition of sexual excess. Coming to the throne in her early thirties and free of the ties of marriage (unless there is any truth in the rumour that she married a Cossack peasant who sang in the Imperial chapel choir), she used her autocratic powers to ensure a constant sexual roundabout. Foreign ambassadors at the Imperial court reported that she abandoned herself to 'every excess of intemperance and lubricity' and noted that she had 'not an ounce of nun's flesh about her'. It would appear that a nun might have been the only piece of flesh that she did not make a grab for. It was not just the quantity of liaisons that marked Elizabeth's reign but also the variety. The Empress had a marked tendency towards transvestism. A feature of court balls became the requirement of courtiers to don the clothes of the opposite sex, while the Tsarina's favourite predilection was to wear the garb of a Dutch sailor (oddly enough, a disguise also used by her father).

---

*General Phillippe Pétain, the victor of both the battlefield and the bedroom*

AFTER TWO YEARS of the First World War, French morale had reached rock bottom. The bloodiest of the innumerable battles of 1916 was taking place around the vital fortress of Verdun, whose defence soon began to symbolise the entire French will to fight. A man of exceptional quality was needed to command the French forces; the man chosen was General Phillippe Pétain. The problem was that Pétain could not be found. Whilst armies fought to the death at the front, staff officers scoured Paris, seeking to inform the General of his momentous appointment. Mindful of Pétain's reputation as a ladies' man, they finally ran the white-haired, sixty-year-old to ground in the Hotel Terminus at the Gare du Nord, where he was happily ensconced with his mistress. The management initially denied that Pétain was a resident, but the staff officers found the General's boots (and a pair of lady's slippers) outside a bedroom door. Eventually Pétain emerged and told the officer to find himself a room for the night; he would complete his current engagement and take up his appointment in the morning.

EMMA HAMILTON'S place in history was assured by her affair with Admiral Nelson, but although he was by far her most famous lover, he was by no means the first. She arrived in London in 1779, aged about fifteen, and soon put her exceptional beauty to good use. She found employment at Dr Graham's 'Temple of Hymen', which was a cross between a brothel, strip joint and health club. Not surprisingly, she caught the eye of one of her clients, Sir Harry Fetherstonhaugh, and was subsequently established as his mistress in a love nest in the country. She provided him with a child before transferring her affections to Charles Greville who, in turn, passed her on to his uncle, Sir William Hamiliton. Although her senior by some thirty years, Hamilton married her and together they set up home in Naples where Sir

*The young and, apparently, demure Emma Hamilton*

William was the British Ambassador. They appear to have been relatively content until, in 1798, Nelson arrived on the scene. An affair soon blossomed between Lady Hamilton and the Admiral that was conducted with scant regard for social convention. This state of affairs was greatly facilitated by Sir William's naive faith in the 'purity' of their friendship, a faith that was to last until his death in 1803. But the social disapprobation that had been held in check during their affair was unleashed following Nelson's death at the Battle of Trafalgar in 1805. Emma became an extravagant and poverty-stricken outcast, the unwanted (and now grossly overweight) mistress of a dead hero. She was put in prison for debt and took to the bottle, before fleeing the country to avoid her creditors. She died a broken woman in Calais in 1815.

◆

IN SPITE OF THE NUMBER of sexual skeletons filling their own cupboards, Hitler and his cronies were never slow to use sex scandals as a means of disposing of their political opponents. No better example exists than the manner in which they gained effective control of the German army. Generals von Blomberg and von Fritsch were respectively Minister of Defence and Commander-in-Chief of the army during the mid-1930s, but by 1937 they were showing clear signs of opposition to Hitler's plans. Their removal was therefore deemed essential, but their rank and position precluded the Nazis' usual violent solution. However, von Blomberg to a certain extent dug his own grave by marrying his young secretary, about whom there were rumours of a shady past. A dossier on the bride was collected and passed around the army and Nazi Party hierarchy. With the dissemination of the evidence that Frau von Blomberg had not been a prostitute but had modelled for pornographic photographs, the General was obliged to resign his post. Meanwhile, the Gestapo engineered a smear campaign against von Fritsch, fabricating an extremely flimsy charge of homosexuality. Von Fritsch contested the accusation and, in a military court of honour, he was judged totally innocent of all charges. Nevertheless, Hitler still got what he wanted. The General's professional reputation was ruined, while he emerged an understandably disillusioned man. He resigned on 4 February 1938 (the same day as von Blomberg), and the path was clear for Hitler to win control of Germany's armed forces.

◆

IT IS NO WONDER that Charles II was known as the 'Merry Monarch'. The names of at least thirteen of his mistresses are known to historians, while it is extremely likely that there were many others whose services were rendered either casually or secretly so that their names are not known. The lovers that have been identified are a tribute to Charles's catholic taste in women, who ranged from the English aristocracy (Lady Burton) and the French nobility (Duchess of Châtillon) to London actresses (Nell Gwynne). There also exists a degree of uncertainty about the number of his illegitimate children, but a fair indication of their number is that six of his bastard sons were created Dukes. In spite of his reputation as a lover, Charles's marriage was childless, and his relationship with his wife was a thing of duty and politeness rather than an affair of passion.

*A highly uncharacteristic scene of coyness between Charles II and Nell Gwynne*

*A rare moment of reflection for Byron*

LORD BYRON had all the fame, notoriety and charisma of the twentieth-century's film and pop stars. He also had a sex life that would have provided ideal material for the gossip columnists and more lurid Sunday newspapers. That he spent a month in Gibraltar with his mistress Mrs Smith was none too shocking. His affair with Lady Caroline Lamb, the wife of the politician William Lamb (later to become the Prime Minister, Lord Melbourne), was, however, the talk of London. The fact that Lady Caroline was decidedly unbalanced soon dampened Byron's ardour and finally extinguished it when she publically made a suicide attempt after he snubbed her. But there was to be no shortage of gossip about Byron's love life, even without Lady Caroline. His marriage failed after a year and there was much talk that he had an incestuous relationship with his half-sister. All this scandal finally drove Byron from England to the waiting arms of a host of Italian ladies who consoled him in his exile.

FOR SHEER RATE of sexual activity, Ibn Saud, the founder of Saudi Arabia, takes some beating. Although helped by Islamic law and tradition, he nonetheless exhibited a healthy passion for the opposite sex and almost single-handedly created a thriving royal dynasty. Permitted to have four wives at any one time and aided by an uncomplicated divorce procedure (just tell her before witnesses three times that she was divorced and the deed was done), Ibn Saud was married at fifteen, had clocked up seventy-five marriages by the time he was thirty-five and had probably tied the knot with some 300 ladies by the time he died. To supplement his official spouses he also indulged in extra-marital liaisons with his numerous concubines and slave girls. Forty-four sons survived childhood (with no record of child deaths and female children) who carried on the remarkable family name.

◆

GEORGE III was an uninspired but generally conscientious king, the history of his reign being dominated by the loss of the American colonies thereby giving him the somewhat unjustified reputation of being a 'bad' ruler. In fact, George was an unlucky king who was always conscious of his regal responsibilities and endeavoured to do the right thing. Even his marriage was an affair of state rather than the heart. His queen, Charlotte of Mecklenburg-Strelitz, was dim and ugly but this did not prevent George fathering a record fifteen legitimate children. It has, however, been speculated that his performance was an act of willpower rather than desire and that the strain of fulfilling his marital duties added greatly to his incipient insanity.

IMPERIAL VIENNA with its waltzes, 'Blue Danube' and gay hussars was a lively place in the nineteenth century. The ruling Habsburg dynasty entered into the spirit of things even down to the usually timid Archduke Ferdinand Maximilian, whose speciality appears to have been a nice line in female impersonation. On one occasion, this royal drag artist had himself introduced at court as the Princess of Modena. On another occasion, dressed in a woman's nightdress, he treated the guards at the Schoenbrunn Palace to renditions from Bellini's *La Sonnambula* in the style of the famous soprano Jenny Lind, giving his performance from the Palace rooftops to an audience of highly amused soldiers.

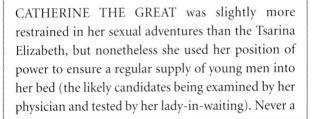

CATHERINE THE GREAT was slightly more restrained in her sexual adventures than the Tsarina Elizabeth, but nonetheless she used her position of power to ensure a regular supply of young men into her bed (the likely candidates being examined by her physician and tested by her lady-in-waiting). Never a

*Catherine the Great sporting a provocatively positioned fashion accessory on her ample bosom*

great beauty, as she grew older she became increasingly fat, but this scarcely impeded her amorous liaisons. Even in her later years, young guardsmen were always found to push the total of her lovers beyond the half century.

# FAILURES

IT HAD ALWAYS BEEN one of the first duties of a monarch to secure the dynasty by producing a number of suitable heirs. The consequence of this was that any infertile king or queen was classed as a failure, and knew themselves to be such. Perhaps the most prolific but unlucky breeder was Queen Anne, who spent most of her married life in a state of pregnancy. She married Prince George of Denmark in 1683 and together they ensured that Anne was preg-

*Queen Anne understandably feels the need to lean on something as she awaits her next pregnancy*

nant every year until 1700. But in spite of their sterling efforts, none of their children survived. Besides twelve miscarriages, one child was stillborn and five others died of dropsy at an early age. It is ironic that the most fecund of the Stuarts should have been the last, her failure to produce an heir resulting in the arrival of the Hanoverian dynasty on the throne.

———————◆———————

PUBLIUS HELVETIUS PERTINAX followed the Emperor Commodus as ruler of the Roman Empire. It was not a popular decision – with Pertinax. He was chosen by the soldiers to be their Emperor but he did not want the job and tried to foist the 'honour' onto several other members of the Senate. Pertinax's reluctance was well-founded, for less than three months later he was killed by the very soldiers who had chosen him. There then followed what can only be described as the sale of the millennium when the palace guards put the Empire up for auction. The winning bid came from Marcus Didius Julianus, who offered 6,200 denarii to each of the Praetorian Guards. It seems that the only person who did not realise that the whole affair was a farce was the new Emperor. The people of Rome pelted him with stones whenever he left the palace and there were soon armies marching from the provinces to depose him. It did not take too long before even Julianus saw which way the wind was blowing. At first he tried to buy off the rebels, then, in desperation, he fortified his palace against attack. Little more than two months after making his purchase, Julianus had lost his throne, becoming the victim of yet another assassination by the Imperial bodyguard. He had scarcely got value for money.

◆

FATE SOMETIMES makes people born failures; everything they touch turns to stone. One such unfortunate was James Edward Stuart, the son of King James II. Because his father was unpopular and few wanted to have him as an heir to the throne, rumours were circulated that the King's son had been smuggled into the royal maternity room in a bedwarming pan, replacing the Queen's stillborn child. A slur that he was an imposter surrounded him thereafter, providing an inauspicious start to a career that was to become a catalogue of failure. Six months after his son's birth, James II was deposed, and father and son went into exile in France. For the rest of his life, James Edward made a series of ill-timed, half-hearted attempts to win back the crown of England. In 1708 he caught measles just before his followers launched an invasion on his behalf, and the sickly leader of the rebellion merely sailed around the British Isles without landing. A better-organised effort in 1715 might have brought more success, but James Edward's lack of leadership and weak character contributed to the rebellion's defeat. After spending six weeks in his homeland he resumed his exile. Even his private life was a disaster, for, although his wife provided him with two sons, their marriage was such that she was moved to take the extreme step of spending two years in a convent away from her husband. It was with much relief that James Edward Stuart handed over the irksome task of saving the Jacobite cause to his son, 'Bonnie Prince Charlie'. Now, out of the limelight, 'the King across the water' spent the rest of his life in Rome, a dull, devout and dreary failure to his end in 1766.

◆

HOWEVER EXTENSIVE his training and however deep his experience, the undercover agent is always liable to falter under the unbearable strain put on a man's nerves by a life of constant tension. During the last war, General Delestraint, an officer appointed by de Gaulle to lead the French Resistance's Secret Army, was travelling through occupied Paris. It had been arranged that he spend the night at a safe house, and the General was pleasantly surprised when an attractive woman answered his knock at the door. His delight, however, rapidly turned to despair when he realised that he had completely forgotten the password. Both he and the woman knew the rules and, after a few minutes' idle chat, he was obliged to leave without entering the apartment, instead having to take a room at a nearby hotel. But now the agent's night turned from a nuisance into a disaster; in his flustered state, he signed the register with his real name and, as a result, was arrested early next day. His night of mental chaos was to cost him his life: he was taken to Germany and died in Dachau concentration camp.

*The classroom dunce fights his last battle*

GENERAL GEORGE ARMSTRONG CUSTER'S place in history derives from his disastrous command of the US 7th Cavalry at the Battle of the Little Big Horn in 1876. But an intimation of 'Long Hair's' notable lack of military talent came very early in his career when, in 1861, he graduated from West Point Military Academy, recording an inauspicious thirty-fourth place out of a class of thirty-four.

# DRINK AND DRUGS

DRINKING HABITS have changed over the centuries. The eighteenth century was perhaps the most bibulous, but by the time of the Napoleonic Wars attitudes were beginning to change. Both Napoleon and his adversary, the Duke of Wellington, were con-

*Wellington boots prove their usefulness in helping the Duke to stand up after a night on the town*

sidered by their contemporaries to be very moderate drinkers. But what appeared to be a small amount in the 1800s is today the intake of someone with a drink problem. Observers wrote that Wellington only had four or five glasses of wine at dinner and about a pint of claret afterwards. Napoleon was remarkable for drinking even less, taking a mere half-pint of claret with each meal and even cutting this down to a couple of glasses of watered wine when in exile on St. Helena.

IT WAS SAID of the Roman Emperor Maximinius Thrax that he liked a glass of wine. In fact, he is reported to have drunk a jug every day. But what seems on the surface to have been a fairly normal intake becomes something quite remarkable when it is noted that the jug in question was a Capitoline amphora which held forty-six pints of wine. Roman historians wrote that at times of stress Maximinius drank himself into a stupor – one cannot, however, help being rather surprised that anything gave him much cause for concern, given his daily consumption of nearly six gallons of wine.

THE ASSASSINATION of President Abraham Lincoln in April 1865 created a huge empty space in American politics. It fell to his Vice-President,

*President Johnson seems to be having a problem focusing but steadies himself on a conveniently positioned table*

Andrew Johnson, to attempt the impossible task of filling the gap and stepping into the great man's shoes. But the task soon proved too much for him. Already unpopular with many of Washington's politicians, Johnson eased the immense pressure on himself by a steady intake of alcohol. The most traumatic experience looked certain to be his inauguration, so he fortified himself with medicinal whisky and, as a result, faced the ceremony in a state of alcoholic equanimity (albeit with notably slurred speech). His inability to speak coherently, to remember the oath of office, or to walk in a straight line, were later explained as the effects of a recent 'illness'.

THE REAL CALAMITY JANE was nothing like the freckled, singing and dancing tomboy portrayed by Doris Day in the musical film of the Wild West's most famous cowgirl. Virtually the only concession towards feminity displayed by Jane in real life was the rumour that she was, at one time, Wild Bill Hickok's lover. Apart from that one exception, she

*Calamity Jane juggling with her pistol – a feat not to be attempted during one of her regular periods of inebriation*

spent most of her time proving that she could out-shoot, outfight and outdrink any male master of these dubious activities. Her later years saw her health ruined by drink and, in spite of several attempts to help her, she became a liability to her friends. Money raised in a benefit to provide for her old age was spent on a mammoth alcoholic binge, and a job at the Pan-American Exposition did not survive a bar-room brawl and her assault on two policemen. She lived up to her name right to the end and, in 1902, only a year before her death, she is reported to have shot up a bar in Montana.

◆

ALBERT EDWARD, Prince of Wales, later King Edward VII, was a famous connoisseur of wine, food and women. Of the three pursuits, drink was per-haps the least essential, and the Prince dispensed with long drinking sessions after meals in favour of a quick glass of brandy and the ladies' company. Nevertheless, Edward usually ensured that he had ample supplies to slake his thirst. He was certainly well prepared for a trip on the River Nile in 1868, accompanied by some twenty guests. Provisions for the party on their six-week cruise included 3,000 bottles of champagne, 4,000 bottles of claret, cases of sherry, beer and liqueurs, and 20,000 bottles of soda water. This reservoir of liquid sustenance filled an entire supply boat, but doubtless helped to make the Sphinx even more enigmatic than usual.

*King Edward VII looks none too pleased with what the spa town of Marienbad has to offer in the way of liquid refreshment*

◆

THE AMERICAN WRITER Edgar Allan Poe easily qualifies for a place in virtually every section of this book. He was a failure both as a university student and a military cadet, being thrown out of the University of Virginia (after only one term) for bad gambling debts, and dismissed from West Point (after a year) because of his 'gross neglect of duty'. He was frequently ill and given to bouts of insanity

*The young Queen Victoria before her partiality for drink sent her weight soaring upwards*

that were characterised by violent outbursts, leading to a suspicion that he had committed a murder in 1841. His sex life was also colourful, including, amongst amongst other aberrations, a marriage to his fourteen-year-old cousin. But, above all, his life and death were dominated by his dependence on drink and drugs. He ended his days in 1849, having been found semi-conscious in a Baltimore saloon. Sadly his last words, 'Lord help my poor soul', were scarcely worthy of his previously outstanding performance in all other categories.

IN SPITE OF HER later puritanical image, in her youth Queen Victoria was by no means teetotal. Although beer 'did not agree with her' and champagne made her 'giddy', she was most partial to sweet ale and negus, a beverage similar to sweet mulled wine. But as her weight soared to nearly nine stones, the diminutive Queen (she was barely five feet tall) determined to diet and cut down on her boozing.

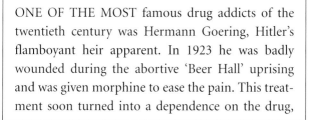

ONE OF THE MOST famous drug addicts of the twentieth century was Hermann Goering, Hitler's flamboyant heir apparent. In 1923 he was badly wounded during the abortive 'Beer Hall' uprising and was given morphine to ease the pain. This treatment soon turned into a dependence on the drug, which was fuelled by his depression at the coup's failure and his enforced exile from Germany. Finally, in September 1925 Goering was admitted to an asylum in Sweden (his wife's native country) and was obliged to undergo a six-month cure for his addiction.

*Hermann Goering, in spite of appearances, photographed **before** he became a drug addict*

Anti-Nazi propaganda certainly made use of Goering's drug addiction and it is therefore difficult fully to assess whether he really managed to kick the habit. Albert Speer intriguingly recalled a story that Goering had been sued for 'improperly administering morphine' to a woman in a night club whose dress had caught fire. Goering had injected her with morphine to relieve the pain of her burns, but his 'patient' subsequently took him to court in order to gain compensation for the needle scar. Less fanciful, however, are the reports that Goering developed an addiction to paracodeine, but, although he was observed munching pills as if they were sweets, it seems likely that they contained only a very small drug dosage.

# DEATHS

KING JOHN of England was a gourmand in an age when large appetites were common. But John's love of food and drink was ultimately to prove his undoing. As his kingdom collapsed into war and chaos, John grew fatter and fatter. Great pains were taken to ensure that the finest wines were always available at each stop on the royal tour and, at the time when all good Catholics refrained from eating meat on Fridays, John ate beef every day, hoping that gifts for the poor would excuse this infraction of ecclesiastical rules. In October 1216 John finally reaped the fruits of his over-indulgence by dying at Newark after a short illness. The source of his malady had been given as a surfeit of either peaches or lamphries (eel-like fish) washed down with too much new cider.

*King John takes a break from compulsive eating in order to kill the next course*

PERHAPS THE MOST famous death of the Third Reich was the murder of the twenty-three-year-old Horst Wessel. Bringing the full weight of the Nazi propaganda machine to bear, Joseph Goebbels made Wessel into the movement's most famous martyr. A nondescript poem, written by Wessel, was set to music and became the official marching song of the Party, while its author posthumously came to

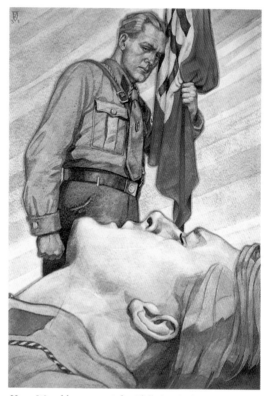

*Horst Wessel bows out. A fancifully heroic depiction of a singularly inglorious death*

embody the finest ideals of Nazi manhood. Needless to say, the legend was almost entirely a fabrication. In fact, Wessel was a down-and-out, failed student who had joined the Nazi Party in 1926 and later enrolled in the SA. He steadily became disenchanted with the movement and resigned from his 'Brownshirt' unit so that he could spend more time with his prostitute mistress. Nevertheless, in February 1930, Wessel became involved in a fight with a gang of left-wing activists and was shot by Ali Hohler. It is, however, in question whether Wessel died defending his Nazi beliefs, for it seems likely that Hohler, the former pimp of Wessel's lover, was motivated by something more basic than political ideology.

◆

ON 12 AUGUST 1822 Lord Castlereagh, Foreign Secretary and Leader of the House of Commons, cut his throat with a penknife that he had bought from a street trader for a shilling. It was widely known that Castlereagh had been under a great deal of stress for a considerable period of time, and was showing signs of what we now recognise as a nervous breakdown. But it was not merely affairs of state that drove the Foreign Secretary to suicide. It had come to light that Castlereagh was the victim of a blackmail plot which, together with the burdens of government, made him kill himself. It transpires that Castlereagh occasionally enjoyed the company of prostitutes whom he picked up on his way home to St James's Square from the Houses of Parliament. One day in 1819 he was propositioned. He accepted and accompanied the whore to a nearby room. It was a set-up. Once in the bedroom, the prostitute revealed 'herself' to be a boy wearing women's clothing and, simultaneously, 'witnesses' rushed in. The gang threatened to denounce him as a homosexual (a punishable crime as well as a social stigma) unless he gave them money. For the next three years one of the most powerful men in Britain was the victim of continuous harassment by a gang of London crooks. For Castlereagh the only escape was death.

———————◆———————

ONE DAY IN OCTOBER 1920, King Alexander of Greece took his dog for a walk in the grounds of his palace at Tatoi, near Athens. The King was a tragic figure who had been coerced into taking his father's place on the throne but whose wife was denied the rank and privileges of a queen. During the course of their melancholy promenade, the King's dog became involved in a fight with the pet monkey of the vineyard keeper. Alexander tried to separate the two animals, but for his pains was bitten in the ankle by the monkey. His injury did not appear too serious and, after the wound was dressed, he walked back to the palace. Two days later, however, blood poisoning set in, and shortly afterwards the king died – a fatal victim of kindness to animals.

FIFTY YEARS before the birth of Christ, Rome was enjoying one of those golden eras that broke through the mire of palace revolutions, decadence and violence. Three of Rome's most able sons formed a triumvirate: Gnaeus Pompeius, Gaius Julius Caesar, and Marcus Licinius Crassus. Of the three, Crassus was the least talented but, as the richest man in Rome, he was an essential part of any government. He suppressed Spartacus's revolt, but his attempt to emulate his colleagues' victories on the field of battle failed abysmally. While Pompey and Caesar met success in nearly every engagement, Crassus's army was soundly defeated by the Parthians at the battle of Carrhae and its general captured. His execution was a gruesome, if apt, end to a capitalist trying to be a soldier; his Parthian captors poured molten gold down his throat.

———————◆———————

RICHARD THE LIONHEART was not the man that popular history would have us believe. In recent years his chivalric crown has slipped somewhat as historians have pinpointed his violence, greed, homosexuality and poor kingship (he was only in England for two short periods during a ten-year reign). But at least he played the part of the hero when fatally wounded at the siege of Chaluz. An arrow struck him in the shoulder and, although at first his condition was not serious, the wound became gangrenous. It is recorded that as his death approached, the King ordered that the archer who had fired the arrow (and who was now a prisoner) be brought to him. Magnanimously, Richard gave his killer a free pardon and a gift of money before he finally expired on 6 April 1199. If that was the end of the 'Lionheart', it was soon the end of the archer, for Richard's men did not obey his orders. He was taken to the dead King's sister, who instructed that the unfortunate be mutilated, flayed and torn apart by horses.

*Richard the Lionheart doing what he did best*

*'The Lady in Black'* – Queen Victoria still in widow's weeds years after Albert's death

PERHAPS THE MOST famous death of the nine-teenth century was the demise of Prince Albert of Saxe-Coburg-Gotha, the husband of Queen Victoria. The Prince Consort died in December 1861 after a month's illness; his wife's mourning was to last rather longer – forty years. The cause of Albert's death was typhoid fever contracted at Windsor Castle, where the drainage and sanitation system had been little improved since the Middle Ages. However, Queen Victoria had other ideas about how her husband had succumbed. She believed that Albert had died of worry and grief over the revela-tion that the Prince of Wales had taken a mistress while serving with the Army in Ireland.

*Queen Anne Boleyn whose necklace might have
served as a handy sighting mark for the executioner*

ON 19 MAY 1536 Queen Anne Boleyn was executed at the Tower of London. She had been found guilty of a variety of trumped-up charges (including incest, adultery and conspiracy to poison), but her real crime had been a failure to provide Henry VIII with a male heir. The law provided that she be either burnt or beheaded at the King's pleasure, but Anne requested that, instead of the English custom of using an axe, she be executed in the French style, with a sword, and Henry acceded to this bizarre preference. England, however, was not exactly full of trained swordsmen queuing up to carry out the job, and the execution was therefore postponed for twenty-four hours to allow a professional from Calais to arrive. This executioner was obviously worth waiting for, because his two-handed sword severed the Queen's head with one blow.

THEY FIRST REALISED that something was wrong when Stalin did not ring for his dinner to be brought to him. But so great was the fear inspired by the Soviet ruler that his guards were frightened to go in and see what had happened. In order to evade his wrath, they sent an old maid into his room to check on him, but even when she reported that the great man was lying unconscious on the floor, they were still uncertain about what action to take. Finally, after much debate, a party of high-ranking Praesidium officials agreed to accept the responsibility, and Stalin was, at last, examined by doctors. They diagnosed a brain haemorrhage caused by cerebral arteriosclerosis and high blood pressure, and confided that his chances of survival were slim. They were right. On 5 March 1953, 'Uncle Joe', the murderer of millions, passed away.

BY A.D. 37 the Emperor Tiberius was very old and extremely ill but he refused to die. After a series of fits and hallucinations it seemed that the long struggle against death was over. His body lay lifeless and his face seemed the face of a corpse. But just as his successor, Caligula, was accepting congratulations as the new emperor, Tiberius sat up and asked for something to eat. If he expected food, he was disappointed, for the nearest he got to swallowing anything were the cushions thrust into his face that quickly suffocated him.

HENRY V is remembered as a paragon of medieval valour, immortalised in Shakespeare's play. The bard concludes his story with Henry showing himself to be as adept at wooing his bride as he had been at beating the French army at Agincourt. Perhaps it is as well that Shakespeare finished the tale there, for Henry's death ill-befitted his heroic image as the warrior king. He died in 1422, not in battle, nor even in England, but at Vincennes, near Paris, a victim of the ignoble disease of dysentery. It was a singularly inappropriate and premature end for a monarch who, it has been said, held the leadership of all Christendom within his grasp. In fact, even as the thirty-five-year-old sovereign lay dying, he was making plans to lead a new crusade to the Holy Land.

LOUIS XI OF FRANCE reigned for sixty years from 1423 to 1483 but any belief that he had had a good innings would have been wide of the mark. In his later life he became terrified at the prospect of death and went to great lengths to 'buy' himself more time. He tried to purchase the intercession of the saints, spending 200,000 francs on a silver screen for St Martin of Tours and making numerous gifts to shrines and cathedrals in France, Italy and Germany. He even enlisted the aid of a Calabrian hermit who left his cave to visit the king but the only comfort he offered the anxious Louis was 'trust in God'.

LOIS · · XI ·

*Louis XI looking suitably pious*

# VIOLENCE

*The face of the 'Monster'*

THE EMPEROR Marcus Aurelius, a sensible, deep-thinking ruler, was succeeded by his son, Commodus. Nicknamed the 'Monster', Commodus was a sexual psychopath and sadist who ruled as if he was trying to compensate for the sanity of his father's reign. An early intimation of his character came when, aged twelve, he ordered that a slave be thrown into the palace furnace because the Imperial bath water was too hot. As Emperor, however, the scale of his cruelty and sexual excess was increased, with 300 boys and 300 girls press-ganged into his bi-sexual harem. When he tired of sexual frolics, Commodus turned to violence, dressing cripples as snakes and then using them as archery targets.

RICHARD I is usually credited with being a soldier of great chivalry who honoured and respected his Moslem adversaries, the Saracens. However, the 'Lionheart' was not above butchering over 2,000 Arab prisoners that he had captured after the fall of Acre to the Crusader army in July 1191. He did not kill the captives immediately, but had them slaughtered a month later, after negotiations with Saladin, the Saracen leader, had broken down.

THE WARS OF THE ROSES raged virtually unchecked from 1455 to 1485. Ostensibly, it was a struggle for the throne of England fought out between two rival noble families, York and Lancaster, but men swopped sides as their sentiments and the tide of war dictated. The upshot of this protracted conflict was that the English medieval aristocracy was all but wiped out. So violent was the age that death could come from any direction – even from a comrade-in-arms. At the battle of Tewkesbury in 1471, the Lancastrian army was defeated. As the Yorkists launched their final charge, the Duke of Somerset rode up to his fellow Lancastrian, Lord Wenlock. Instead of commiserating, he declared that Wenlock had failed to help him in the battle and, with a single blow of his battle-axe, he split the nobleman's head in two. But Somerset did not long outlive his victim – he was captured by the Yorkists and beheaded a couple of days later.

◆

THE INDIAN MUTINY of 1857 was notable for the appalling atrocities committed by both sides, each inflamed by the stimulants of religion, fear and drink. The most infamous deed of the war was the massacre at Cawnpore, when European women and children, held captive after the men had been slaughtered, were themselves murdered. The mutineers had taken fright at the approach of a British relief force and, in their panic, had hacked to

THE HOUSE (NATIVE) IN WHICH OUR WOMEN WERE SLAUGHTERED BY ORDER OF NANA SAHIB ON 16TH JULY. 1857. From A DRAWING ON THE SPOT BY LIEUT CRUMP. R.A

*The scene of the crime and the British Army's retribution*

death some 300 prisoners, disposing of their bodies in the river or down a well. They scarcely made any effort to hide the massacre and, after Cawnpore's recapture, the British troops were incensed by the scenes of carnage that met their eyes. Thereafter, few mutineers were taken prisoner, save for those whose lives were spared only to allow for punishment before death. Brigadier-General Neill ordered that captured mutineers were to be taken to the scene of the massacre where they were forced to lick clean a square foot of the room's blood-stained floor. When this task was completed, usually with the encouragement of the lash, the miscreants were taken out and hanged.